The Magnificent Gift

The Path to Joy and Peace

Nancy Moradian

WESTBOW
PRESS®
A DIVISION OF THOMAS NELSON
& ZONDERVAN

Scripture taken from the Holy Bible, NEW INTERNATIONAL VERSION®. Copyright © 1973, 1978, 1984, 2011 by Biblica, Inc. All rights reserved worldwide. Used by permission. NEW INTERNATIONAL VERSION® and NIV® are registered trademarks of Biblica, Inc. Use of either trademark for the offering of goods or services requires the prior written consent of Biblica US, Inc.

Scripture taken from the New Century Version. Copyright © 2005 by Thomas Nelson, Inc. Used by permission. All rights reserved.

WestBow Press books may be ordered through booksellers or by contacting:

WestBow Press
A Division of Thomas Nelson & Zondervan
1663 Liberty Drive
Bloomington, IN 47403
www.westbowpress.com
1 (866) 928-1240

ISBN: 978-1-9736-1075-5 (sc)
ISBN: 978-1-9736-1076-2 (e)

Library of Congress Control Number: 2017919185

Print information available on the last page.

WestBow Press rev. date: 1/31/2018

I dedicate this book to my daughter Megan
to enjoy and live life to the fullest.

Once there was a young man who wondered, "Of all the secrets in the universe, what is the secret of happiness and peace?"

In his search for happiness, he skied on the snowy tops of majestic mountains in Austria. He hiked on safari through dense, humid jungles in Africa. He rode a raft down the brisk, white waters of the Colorado River. He ventured on deep-sea diving expeditions and was enthralled by the colorful fish. He traveled near and far looking for something that would give him that special feeling of happiness within.

God, you are my God. I search for you. I thirst for you like someone in a dry, empty land where there is no water. Because your love is better than life, I will praise you (Psalms 63:1, 3 NCV).

Throughout his journey, he met many people of different cultures and asked, "What is the secret of happiness and peace?" He heard many different answers. Some people said love. Others said children. Still others said it was a nice place to live or work you enjoy. But the man was not satisfied with the answers people gave him, so he continued on.

On his journey, he immersed himself in the beauty of nature. He hiked in parks among the wildlife and plant life. He gazed at fountains holding cool, flowing water and shapely statues. He meditated in quiet places hoping to receive an answer about where to find happiness and peace. He enjoyed the outdoors, but still he did not find the answer.

The Lord will always lead you. He will satisfy your needs in dry lands and give strength to your bones. You will be like a garden that has much water, like a spring that never runs dry (Isaiah 58:11 NCV).

He read many books—old books and new books, red books and blue books. He read the best newspapers and magazines. He hoped to find the secret of true happiness tucked away in their pages. He learned much, but he was not any happier.

But if any of you needs wisdom, you should ask God for it. He is generous and enjoys giving to all people, so he will give you wisdom (James 1:5 NCV).

The man had many wonderful friends and companions. He hoped they could provide insight into what real happiness is. He asked, "Do you know the true secret to happiness and peace? One friend had a clever sense of humor and made him laugh. A few other friends shared their opinions on politics and world peace. And others discussed education, finances, and health.

But the man was no closer to finding an answer to his question. He met famous people and inquired about their secrets of happiness and peace. *They are successful*, he thought. *Certainly they must have some wisdom to share with me.* Their answers focused on money, status, and achievements. He was as frustrated as ever.

Jesus said, "Don't let your hearts be troubled. Trust in God and trust in me" (John 14:1 NCV).

The man was in excellent physical condition. He slammed balls in racquetball courts. He tossed balls through basketball hoops. He lifted weights at a health club. Still he was not happy. The man ate nutritional foods. He ran. He swam. He watched his weight.

He looked in the mirror and liked what he saw. He wore the right clothes. He dyed his hair so he would look handsome. He felt proud of his appearance. Still, he did not feel happy.

The man had many interests and hobbies. He golfed with friends at a beautiful course. He volunteered at a local hospital. He led scouting trips for young boys. He collected stuffed animals for his antique collection. He traded. He bought. He sold. He enjoyed adding to his collection. But he did not feel fulfilled.

Do not store treasures for yourselves here on earth where moths and rust will destroy them and thieves will break in and steal them. But store your treasures in heaven where they cannot be destroyed by moths or rust and where thieves cannot break in and steal them. Your heart will be where your treasure is (Matthew 6:19–21 NCV).

The man engaged in several different careers. He was an engineer, a scientist, and an artist. His work did not make him feel happy. He had a big, beautiful home; shiny cars; and expensive stereos and cameras. He sailed across the rolling sea on a large sailboat. He surfed with friends. He danced and had fun. He sang and wrote songs. But somehow the good times quickly passed away leaving nothing but a memory. Nothing the man did brought more than fleeting happiness. The man felt sad in his heart. His best friend stood by him and encouraged him, "One day you will find happiness."

God is our protection and our strength. He always helps in times of trouble. The Lord All Powerful is with us; The God of Jacob is our defender (Psalms 46:1, 11 NCV).

He wondered if marriage was the path to happiness. He married a beautiful woman. The woman had a vibrant personality and positive spirit. The man was truly in love. He felt waves of pleasure caress him daily. He finally thought he had found what he was looking for. Still he was not happy. Something was missing.

People may make plans in their minds, but only the Lord can make them come true. Depend on the Lord in whatever you do, and your plans will succeed (Proverbs 16:1, 3 NCV).

The man and woman had a child together, a beautiful girl blessed with a cheerful spirit. She brought them many magical moments of laughter and joy. The family visited many places together—the zoo, the park, the museum. They were all grateful for all the wonderful times they shared. Was this what happiness is all about?

Every good action and every perfect gift is from God. These good gifts come down from the Creator of the sun, moon, and stars, who does not change like their shifting shadows (James 1:17 NCV).

As time went on, the child grew into a charming young lady. She was bright and perceptive.

One day she asked, "Daddy, what's the secret of happiness and peace?" The man replied, "I'm still searching for it myself. Just when I think I've found it, something happens and it escapes my grasp." The man loved his daughter and his wife. He was successful and prosperous. He had many of the material things in life that others often wish for. He was lucky. Yet the man believed he was still missing something. What was it?

I am the Lord, the God of every person on the earth. Nothing is impossible for me (Jeremiah 32:27 NCV).

Years passed, the man aged, and he became ill and exhausted. After countless years of stressful searching, he was no further ahead than when he had started. The man felt annoyed. The gnawing, empty feeling had been present for over thirty years. But he would not give up. He continued to look for happiness and peace.

But the wisdom that comes from God is first of all pure, then peaceful, gentle, and easy to please. This wisdom is always ready to help those who are troubled and to do good for others. It is always fair and honest (James 3:17 NCV).

One day the man was surprised to find himself in the hospital. He had been in an auto accident and was badly injured. As he lay in bed healing, God spoke to him in a soft whisper. God told him, "The gift of happiness cannot be found in the external world. It does not come wrapped in beautiful paper. Happiness and peace are wrapped in my love for you. You may receive them at any time. Come to me, and I will give you a gift that will provide for everything you'll ever need, and it will last forever. Many people have already received my gift. They chose to receive my son, Jesus Christ, and allowed him to live in their hearts forever. It has been the wisest choice they have ever made."

Here I am! I stand at the door and knock. If anyone hears my voice and opens the door, I will come in and eat with him, and he with me (Revelation 3:20 NIV).

"The gift I send you is my son, Jesus Christ. This gift is so grand; it is called the magnificent gift," God whispered. "Only you have the power to make yourself happy through receiving Jesus Christ into your heart and your life."

The man was skeptical. He asked, "Will the magnificent gift cause me to give up my freedom?"

"No," God replied. "It is the way to absolute freedom and everlasting life, happiness, and peace."

The man still wasn't sure. Although he was beginning to feel better physically each day, he did not want to commit to something that would require large amounts of time, energy, and effort.

And the angel said unto them Fear not: for, behold, I bring you good tidings of great joy, which shall be to all people. For unto you is born this day in the city of David a Saviour, which is Christ the Lord (Luke 2:10–11 KJV).

few days later the man requested, "Tell me more about this magnificent gift." He was tired of being in a hospital bed and wanted to go home soon.

God replied, "Sure enough, the magnificent gift will benefit all areas of your life. Every aspect of your being will be enriched by accepting and living with Jesus Christ."

And a voice from heaven said, "This is my Son, whom I love; with him I am well pleased" (Matthew 3:17 NIV).

God had observed the man working, playing, and seeking happiness by his own methods. He had great compassion for the man's frustration and pain. God said, "It's easy, child. You simply need to open the door of your heart and invite me in. It will take a few minutes, and the results will be everlasting. You can receive my magnificent gift any time or any place."

The man replied, "I have searched near and far, and I'm so tired of looking for happiness that I've stopped trying."

God replied, "You don't need to try anymore; you can have it now. This minute. Think about it."

How shall we escape, if we neglect so great salvation? (Hebrews 2:3 NIV).

inally, the man was home from the hospital. God turned to the old man and asked, "Are you ready to accept my magnificent gift now?

The man answered with anticipation, "Yes, I'm ready."

God directed the man to one of the bookshelves in his library. "Pull down the big burgundy one."

The man pulled down the dusty Bible he had put on his bookshelf long ago. Inside the front cover was a faded piece of lavender paper that held "The Miracle Prayer." The man folded his hands and read the words aloud.

The Miracle Prayer

Lord Jesus, I come before you just as I am. I am sorry for my sins. I repent of my sins, please forgive me. In your name I forgive all others for what they have done against me. I renounce Satan, the evil spirits, and all their works. I give you my entire self, Lord Jesus, now and forever. I invite you into my life. Jesus, I accept you as my Lord, God, and Savior. Heal me, change me, and strengthen me in body, soul, and spirit. Come, Lord Jesus, cover me with your precious blood and fill me with your Holy Spirit. I love you, Lord Jesus. I praise you, Jesus. I thank you, Jesus. I shall follow you every day of my life. Amen.

For God so loved the world, that he gave his one and only Son, that whoever believes in him should not perish, but have eternal life (John 3:16 NIV).

The man was struck by the truth of the words. He felt a new warmth rise from the depth of his being.

He was overwhelmed by the wisdom he had almost missed. In an instant, the man felt great joy in his heart. The joy of receiving the magnificent gift. The joy of having an identity in Christ. The joy of knowing where he would be going when he died.

You have made known to me the path of life; you will fill me with joy in your presence, with eternal pleasures at your right hand (Psalms 16:11 NIV).

The man wondered why he had not seen the obvious long before. He remembered his fruitless travels around the world. He remembered his search for happiness and peace. He remembered how hard he tried to find the secret. Why have I missed so many precious moments with the Lord searching for what I could have so easily had? All I had to do was open my heart.

I know how to live when I am poor, and I know how to live when I am happy. I have learned the secret of being happy at any time in everything that happens, when I have enough to eat and when I go hungry, when I have more than I need and when I do not have enough. I can do all things through Christ, because he gives me strength (Philippians 4:12–13 NCV).

The man finally discovered the secret. Jesus Christ our Lord and Savior is knocking on the door of your heart. Open that door and the love of God overflows inside us. The man finally knew his Creator. He was listening to the voice of God. The love of Jesus overflowed inside his heart. He felt the safety of the living Christ, dwelling within him. Jesus was all he had ever needed. He truly was the answer.

He said to me: "It is done. I am the alpha and the omega, the beginning and the end. To him who is thirsty I will give to drink without cost from the spring of the water of life" (Revelation 21:6 NIV).

ooking for peace and happiness? Just answer the knock. Open your door. Right now.

Thanks be to God for his indescribable gift! (2 Corinthians 9:15 NIV)

Addendum

The Nine Promises of the Magnificent Gift

J	Jesus Christ will live within you always.
E	You will have everlasting life.
S	The Holy Spirit will guide you.
U	You are unified with believers in Christ.
S	You have received salvation from sin.
I	You have a new identity in Christ.
N	You are now forgiven.
M	You are made anew—transformed.
E	You will have everlasting joy and peace.

Promise 1

Jesus Christ will live within you always. My son, Jesus Christ, will live within you and never leave you. He will protect, strengthen, and enrich you. He will love you always, no matter who or what you are.

The Spirit of truth, the world cannot accept him because it neither sees him nor knows him. But you know him because he lives with you and will be in you (John 14:17 NIV).

Promise 2

You will have everlasting life. You will experience a glorious life in heaven, where there is no pain or suffering. You will know that when you pass from this lifetime, you will continue living with Christ.

I tell you the truth, whoever hears what I say and believes in the one who sent me has eternal life. That person will not be judged guilty but has already left death and entered life (John 5:24 NCV).

Promise 3

The Holy Spirit will guide you. God sent us Jesus so we will have inner peace and security. God gave us his Holy Spirit to guide us and keep us safe. The Holy Spirit will fill you with truth, understanding, and guide you in the right direction toward greater love for your fellow human.

May our Lord Jesus Christ himself and God our Father encourage you and strengthen you in every good thing you do and say. God loved us, and through his grace he gave us a good hope and encouragement that continues forever (2 Thessalonians 2:16–17 NCV).

Promise 4

You are unified with believers in Christ. With Christ you are connected to your fellow man and woman. Treat every man and woman you meet as a brother or sister, as you are just like them.

A person's body is only one thing, but it has many parts. Christ is like that also. Some of us are Jews, and some of us are Greeks. Some of us are slaves, and some are free. But we were all baptized into one body through one Spirit. And we were all made to share in the one Spirit (1 Corinthians 12:12–13 NCV).

Promise 5

You have received salvation from sin. The gift of salvation is absolutely free to all those who believe in Jesus Christ.

All have sinned and are not good enough for God's glory, and all need to be made right with God by his grace, which is a free gift. They need to be made free from sin through Jesus Christ (Romans 3:23–24 NCV).

Promise 6

You have a new identity in Christ. You are totally accepted by God and complete in Christ.

I will give you a new heart and put a new spirit in you (Ezekiel 36:26 NIV).

Promise 7

You are now forgiven.

Be kind and compassionate to one another, forgiving one another, just as in Christ God forgave you (Ephesians 4:32 NIV).

Promise 8

You are made anew—transformed in body and spirit. You are a brand-new person with a new mind, spirit, and body in Christ.

You have begun to live the new life in which you are being made new and are becoming like the one who made you. This new life brings you the true knowledge of God (Colossians 3:10 NCV).

Promise 9

You will have everlasting joy and peace. You will have inner security and joy that will last forever. You will be wonderfully content to be exactly where you are. Whatever occurs during your life journey, you will be able to handle it with Jesus.

The joy of the Lord is your strength (Nehemiah 8:10 NIV).

Reader's Application Guide

1. Are you ready to accept and receive Jesus Christ as your Lord and Savior? Or are you ready to renew your commitment to Jesus Christ as your Lord and Savior?

2. What obstacles or hindrances are preventing you from reaping the benefits of the magnificent gift? Would you like to turn those over to God now?

3. What is the difference between worldly happiness and the joy of Christ in your heart?

4. Do you know anyone that is searching for peace and happiness in all the wrong places? Would you be willing to share this book or these truths with them?